THEN & NOW®

EUREKA

OPPOSITE: This early 1900s view of downtown Eureka shows the Humboldt County Courthouse on the far left, St. Bernard's Church to the right with the Vance Hotel in front of it, and the Revere, Western, and Grand Hotels running along the waterfront from the center to the right. (Courtesy of the Humboldt State University Library.)

THEN & NOW®

EUREKA

Scott H. Brown

In loving memory of my mother, Janet Hubbard Brown.

ISBN 978-0-7385-9676-1

Library of Congress Control Number: 2012942214

Published by Arcadia Publishing
Charleston, South Carolina

Printed in the United States of America

For all general information, please contact Arcadia Publishing:
Telephone 843-853-2070
Fax 843-853-0044
E-mail sales@arcadiapublishing.com
For customer service and orders:
Toll-Free 1-888-313-2665

Visit us on the Internet at www.arcadiapublishing.com

On the Front Cover: The Carson Mansion, designed by the Newsom brothers of San Francisco, is one of the most photographed Victorian homes in California. William Carson had his mansion constructed during a depression in the lumber industry, keeping 100 of his workers employed. The owner of the mansion, The Ingomar Club, has kept the mansion beautifully maintained, and today, it looks nearly identical to when it was completed in 1884. (Then image courtesy of the Humboldt State University Library; now image by the author.)

On the Back Cover: A view down a muddy Second Street sometime in the early 1900s shows that Second and C Streets were then dominated by the Grand Hotel and the Eagle House. The Eagle House opened in 1893, and the Grand Hotel opened in 1890 boasting the finest accommodations that could be found in California north of San Francisco. Because of the competition, the original Eagle House building was split into two sections and moved to accommodate a new three story building, which incorporated the original sections as wings. (Courtesy of the Clarke Historical Museum.)

Contents

ACKNOWLEDGMENTS

I would first like to thank my dad, Herschel Brown, and my grandma Dorcas Hubbard, who both laid the groundwork for my love of history. I would also like to thank Michael Chriswell, Donna Smith, Jason Majors, Gilbert Rodriguez and Natalie Harryman, Rob Kleiner, and Kevin Gibson for their support, help, and encouragement through this process. I also want to thank Amy Perryman and Jared Nelson of Arcadia Publishing. I greatly appreciate the assistance of Joan Berman, special collections librarian at the Humboldt State University Library; Ben Brown of the Clarke Historical Museum; and Linda DeLong of the Humboldt Historical Society. Thank you to Carly Robbins of the Arkley Center for the Performing Arts, Paul McNally of the Ingomar Club, and Terry Coltra of the Indian Development Council for allowing me into their buildings to take several "now" images and for sharing some of the history of their remarkable buildings with me. Finally, I would like to thank Kevin Magladry, Deborah Boots Baskette, Steve Lazar, Lynn McKenna, all of the wonderful people of Remember in Eureka When for their help with photographs and historical information, and Janine Averill for saving the Eureka home that meant so much to my family and me. All of the now images were taken by the author.

Introduction

Humboldt Bay and the surrounding lands had been the ancestral home of the Wiyot, Yurok, Karuk, and Hupa people for over 1,000 years when early European exploration of the area began in 1579. The first known discovery of Humboldt Bay by Europeans occurred in 1806, when the *O'Cain*, a ship from Boston that was hired out to the Russian government with Jonathan Winship at the helm, entered and explored the bay to hunt sea otters. The crew named it the Bay of Rezanov after their Russian sponsor. The bay is a treacherous passage for ships to enter from the Pacific Ocean even today, and due to the geographic features and weather conditions, it is virtually invisible from the sea. It was quickly forgotten about until Shasta County rancher Pierson Reading discovered gold in the Trinity Mountains in 1848, and the Josiah Gregg Expedition rediscovered the bay the following year in search of a water route to the northern gold mines along the Trinity and Klamath Rivers, which had quickly become a center of gold rush activity. In 1850, H.H. Buhne piloted the schooner *Laura Virginia* into the bay, and the men on the ship decided to name it Humboldt Bay after the German scientist and geographer Alexander von Humboldt. Because of its location directly on the protected waters of the newly named Humboldt Bay and the seemingly inexhaustible timber resources surrounding it, the potential of the area was soon realized, and the economy shifted from gold mining to logging, fisheries, and agriculture, which quickly paved the way for the settlement of Eureka, a well-known Greek phrase meaning "I Have Found It!"

The Europeans quickly overwhelmed the native tribes in numbers and eventually cut off all access to their ancestral sources of food and took or destroyed their land. The local tribes fought desperately against displacement, even reaching out to the US government for help to retain control of their land. Despite the efforts of a few government and military officials to assist the natives, they had no success. William Carson is thought to be the only person who ever gave anything to the natives in return for land. The two cultures were in deep conflict, much of it instigated by the settlers through their treatment of the natives. Having exhausted all other options, several of the tribes retaliated in the only other manner they knew. In 1853, the military was called in to protect the settlers, and Fort Humboldt was established; as a young captain, Ulysses S. Grant would serve there. The conflict between the two cultures peaked in 1860, when a small group of white men in a seemingly unprovoked act launched coordinated, simultaneous attacks on several Wiyot villages on Humboldt Bay and the lower Eel River with clubs, knives, and axes, resulting in the deaths of over 150 people, mainly women and children. This was not the first attack, nor was it the last, but it was the most publicized, having been anonymously reported in San Francisco and New York papers (the reports are rumored to have been written by local author Bret Harte). Writers in San Francisco and New York began referring to Eureka as Murderville, and Harte was run out of town, barely escaping with his life. Though the names of those responsible for the Wiyot Massacre were apparently widely known, no legal action was ever taken against them, and after a decade full of murder and intimidation, most of the natives who had once inhabited the area had been killed or removed. In 2004, the City of Eureka returned a large portion of Indian Island back to the Wiyot people.

The lumber industry got off to a rocky start. The Papoose, the first sawmill on Humboldt Bay, opened in 1850 and failed in one year's time, as did several other mills in the area. In 1852, the paddle-wheel steamer *Santa Clara*, loaded with sawmill machinery, left San Francisco with James T. Ryan as the captain, F.S. Duff as the first officer, and John Vance as the quartermaster. After nearly becoming one of the earliest recorded victims of the treacherous passage into the bay, the steamer was driven aground near where First and D Streets are today, and the first successful mill in the county was constructed directly beside the boat using her engines for power to saw spruce, fir, and pine. Only a few years after the first lumber mills on Humboldt Bay had failed, there were seven functioning mills in Eureka and nine countywide, one of them owned by William Carson, a Canadian who brought the first ox team to Humboldt County and had taken over operation of the Hula Mill, the first mill in Humboldt County to saw redwood in 1854. Because of its resistance to rot, redwood was an instantaneous success and soon was being sold at premium prices. By 1855, there were at least 140 lumber schooners operating on Humboldt Bay supplying lumber to cities on the west coast. Five years later, Eureka sawmills were producing over two million feet of lumber per month, and the city was declared "the greatest lumber manufacturing town on the Pacific" by the *Humboldt Times*. With the development of the steam donkey and narrow-gauge railroads, even bigger trees could be felled, and the lumber industry boomed.

Taking advantage of the location along one of the largest protected bodies of water on the west coast, other industries began to spring up. Fisheries and processing plants started to line the waters of the bay as early as 1851, and within five years, they were annually shipping out 2,000 barrels of cured fish and 50,000 pounds of smoked salmon. In 1858, the first of what would be many ships constructed in Eureka was launched into the bay. Despite its isolation, the port of Eureka was one of the busiest in the West. Eureka was incorporated as a town on April 18, 1856; the growing town had carved into the dense forest, and a bustling commercial district now stood along the waterfront. The town was growing at a rapid rate, and saloons and brothels sprang up along the waterfront just as quickly. At one point, a reported 23 bar permits were approved at a single council meeting. Eureka had a well-known reputation for being very rough and wild, and it was well deserved. By 1890, steamships were providing passenger service in and out of Eureka, and all of the towns and mill sites on the bay were linked by ferries. Railroads used to bring logs to mills began to provide limited local passenger service, and Eureka had its own streetcar lines to get around town. With the completion of the Northwestern Pacific Railroad in 1914 and the Redwood Highway in 1922, the town of Eureka, which had been virtually isolated from the outside world for its entire existence, was connected to San Francisco and the other great bay of California.

Today, the city has calmed down, its economy having shifted from logging and fisheries to tourism and the arts, but it retains many reminders of its wild past, having avoided the post-war redevelopment and urban renewal that so many other cities experienced and leaving behind hundreds of examples of 19th- and early-20th-century architecture. Approximately 16 percent of the city's buildings are cataloged as important historical structures, and Old Town is considered one of the nation's best-preserved original Victorian-era commercial districts.

CHAPTER 1

Red Gold

The Excelsior Mill, located on Gunther Island, started off as the Joseph Russ Mill in 1863. It was briefly owned by the California Redwood Company in 1883, but due to legal difficulties, the company was dissolved into the Excelsior Redwood Company, which ran the mill until it closed in the 1890s. (Courtesy of the Humboldt State University Library.)

A late 1920s view looking northeast from the top of the Carson Mansion shows the dry kilns of the Dolbeer and Carson Lumber Company. William Carson had an unobstructed panoramic view of his lumberyard, Humboldt Bay, and the main part of Eureka from his tower. Lumber was used in the construction of many local buildings and was also shipped out for the construction of many landmark buildings such as the Hotel Del Coronado in San Diego. (Then image courtesy of Kevin Magladry.)

A shipment of lumber is being loaded onto a train from the Dolbeer and Carson Lumber Company's docks in the late 1920s. The tower of William Carson's Victorian mansion is visible in the distance on the upper left in both photographs. Today, Waterfront Drive cuts through where the train platforms and buildings once stood, and the old, seldom-used railroad tracks now run along the side of the road. (Then image courtesy of Kevin Magladry.)

The Japanese cargo ship *Erie Maru* is being loaded with redwood at the shipping docks of the Dolbeer and Carson Lumber Mill in the late 1920s. The ship was sunk by the US submarine *Sturgeon* on January 11, 1944, about 20 miles east of Saeki, Kyushu. Today, all that remains of the Dolbeer and Carson docks are the posts that once held them up protruding out of Humboldt Bay. (Then image courtesy of Kevin Magladry.)

The large mill and millpond of Hammonds Bayside Mill was located at the foot of Del Norte Street. Andrew Hammond purchased the railroad and sawmill from John Vance in the year 1900. He is credited for his involvement in the creation of the NorthwesternPacificRailroad, whichranfrom1911 through 1933; the northern six miles continued running until 1948. (Then image courtesy of the Humboldt State University Library.)

A neat building constructed entirely of redwood, the offices of the Dolbeer and Carson Lumber Company stood directly across the street from William Carson's Victorian mansion overlooking the mill. Today, the building remains virtually unchanged and is a private office. It is quite possibly the only structure that was once part of the Dolbeer and Carson mill that still exists. (Then image courtesy of Kevin Magladry.)

The Dolbeer and Carson Lumber Company did not need a millpond, as it could dump directly into the bay. Logs were stored in the water because it helped to clean them, and a floating log was much easier to move. Today, a small section of wall near the Samoa Bridge is all that remains of the log dump. (Then image courtesy of Kevin Magladry.)

Looking east from the tower of the Carson Mansion in the late 1920s, the sprawling Dolbeer and Carson Lumber Company mill and yard are seen. The mill operated from 1863 to 1958, and the buildings stood empty for quite some time before being demolished. Today, the Humboldt County Library stands where the stacks of lumber once were stored, and the majority of the mill property is now a public park. (Then image courtesy of Kevin Magladry.)

The Holmes Lumber Company was founded in 1903 by Joseph H. Holmes. On June 21, 1935, more than 200 striking workers demanding reasonable work hours and better pay clashed with police, leaving three workers dead, eight wounded, and more than 100 in jail. After being sold, the mill was gradually shut down. This is now where the Bayshore Mall stands, and ruins of some of the mill buildings still occupy land behind the mall. (Then image courtesy of the Humboldt State University Library.)

A view from the late 1920s shows redwood logs being hoisted from the waters of Humboldt Bay, where they were stored, into one of the mill buildings of the Dolbeer and Carson Lumber Company to be debarked, cut, and sold. Today, the Samoa Bridge, which was completed in 1971, passes directly over the path the logs once took as they were brought to the mill. (Then image courtesy of Kevin Magladry.)

A late 1920s view taken from the top of the Carson Mansion looks northwest at Humboldt Bay, showing a portion of the Dolbeer and Carson Lumber Company shipping docks, Woodley Island, and Indian Island. John Dolbeer invented the donkey engine, also known as the steam donkey, which revolutionized the logging industry, in 1881. The invention of the internal-combustion engine, however, eventually rendered the donkey engine obsolete. (Then image courtesy of Kevin Magladry.)

The heart of the Dolbeer and Carson Lumber Company was located directly on Humboldt Bay. John Dolbeer and William Carson became partners in 1864, and their mill continued operation into the 1950s. Today, very little remains of the mill—mostly posts that once supported large docks poking up out of the bay and old foundations peeking through the grass and brush of what is now Halverson Park. (Then image courtesy of Kevin Magladry.)

In 1869, Joseph Russ opened his mill on what was then known as Gunther Island. The mill later became the Excelsior Redwood Company. It closed down sometime in the 1890s and burned to the ground in 1915. Today, there is very little standing on the island, which is now known as Indian Island. The MV *Madaket* was launched in 1910 as a passenger ferry and still navigates Humboldt Bay giving harbor cruises. (Then image courtesy of the Humboldt State University Library.)

This view from the top of the Carson Mansion looking west was taken in the late 1920s and shows the office and the shipping docks of the Dolbeer and Carson Lumber Company. Part of the area the docks once occupied is now the Adorni Memorial Recreation Center, a recreation facility, conference room, and gymnasium where many popular annual Eureka events are held. (Then image courtesy of Kevin Magladry.)

A raft of 487,000 board feet floats in Humboldt Bay along the Dolbeer and Carson Lumber Company sometime in the late 1920s. Timber rafting was a common practice in which large quantities of logs were attached and moved across water. This also made log storage much easier in an open body of water with strong currents such as Humboldt Bay. (Then image courtesy of Kevin Magladry.)

The Sturtevant High Humidity Dry Kilns of the Dolbeer and Carson Lumber Company were a new timesaving feature added to the mill around 1920. They were used to remove as much moisture as possible from the lumber after it was cut and were much faster than air drying, which was very difficult to do in the damp Eureka climate. Today, the former location of the kilns is part of Halverson Park (Then image courtesy of Kevin Magladry.)

CHAPTER 2

Life Behind the Redwood Curtain

This birds-eye view looking out across downtown Eureka from around First and A Streets was likely taken from the water tower of the lumber mill that once operated in the area. With only a few exceptions such as the courthouse, which can be seen in the distance, and the imposing Grand Hotel, which is directly in the center, nearly all of these buildings still stand today, making up Historic Old Town Eureka. (Courtesy of the Humboldt State University Library.)

As evidenced in this 1864 picture, the oldest known photograph of the city of Eureka, the city had carved its way into the edge of the forest four blocks away from the waters of Humboldt Bay. The Congregational church building stood at Fourth and G Streets, and the small building in front of it was Pioneer School. This area is now part of the Old Town area of Eureka. (Then image courtesy of the Humboldt State University Library.)

In 1887, plans were made to relocate the small four-room Grant School and construct a large ten-room, three-story schoolhouse to be named Winship School. The rapid growth of Eureka soon overwhelmed the school, and with the completion of a newer modern high school in 1914 and a new junior high school in 1926, the old crumbling building was torn down and replaced by the Eureka Municipal Auditorium. (Then image courtesy of the Humboldt State University Library.)

The Brown School is pictured in 1890. J. Brown, who later became county superintendent of schools, taught in the little schoolhouse built in the 1860s on the corner of H and Sixth Streets. The school building quickly became too small for the growing number of students in Eureka, and in the early 1900s, it was being used for woodworking classes from the severely overcrowded Winship School before being demolished in 1917. (Then image courtesy of the Humboldt State University Library.)

Franklin School opened in 1906 and was located on Myrtle Avenue, which was then bordered with "wild-growing myrtle bushes" and lined with "rickety, knot-holed redwood sidewalks" according to Ben Nichols, a student of the school. In 1913, eucalyptus trees were planted behind the two-story school building, which was later replaced with a larger, more modern building. Today, the eucalyptus trees are still there, and the newer school building now houses the Humboldt County Office of Education. (Then image courtesy of the Humboldt State University Library.)

The St. Joseph Institute opened in 1866 as a young ladies' school and closed after only three years. It was then briefly used as a boarding school before being purchased by Father Patrick Heneberry for use as a seminary. The seminary moved, and the building was taken over by the Sisters of Mercy as a convent and school until 1903. The building was razed in 1920, and the site is now the famous Eureka Inn. (Then image courtesy of the Humboldt State University Library.)

The Sisters of St. Joseph of Orange were established by Mother Bernard Gosselin. In 1912, she and eight sisters left Illinois to establish a school in Eureka. On August 12, 1912, the Sisters established the Nazareth Academy. In 1949, an elementary school was built and staffed by the Sisters, and in 1954, St. Bernard's High School opened. The site of the original Nazareth Academy building is now a sports field. (Then image courtesy of the Humboldt State University Library.)

Very little has changed in these two views taken more than 100 years apart of the Fourth of July festivities on F Street. Most of the buildings were "modernized" at some point in time, and a few still remain that way today, while others have since been restored to their original appearance. (Then image courtesy of the Humboldt State University Library.)

Chinese workers had arrived in California, and they were skilled, efficient, and willing to work for lower wages; for this they were believed to be an economic threat. Deep cultural misunderstandings also made them easy targets. In 1885, when a city councilman was caught in the crossfire of two Chinese gangs and killed near where this photograph was taken, it was the excuse Eureka needed to expel the entire population. (Then image courtesy of the Humboldt State University Library.)

In 1885, two Chinese men began shooting from opposite sides of the street in Chinatown, killing city councilman David Kendall. This sparked public outrage that quickly led to the expulsion of the Chinese people from Eureka, which was followed by a second, lesser-known banishment of 23 Chinese cannery workers in 1906. Today, several rusted train engines are all that remain of the Eureka train station where the events of 1906 occurred. (Then image courtesy of the Humboldt State University Library.)

The Eureka Woolen Mill first opened in 1900. The first few years were a success, but it was to be short-lived, and the mill closed down soon after. It was purchased and reopened in 1916. The mill survived the Great Depression and into the 1950s. When the mill closed, the machinery was sold, and the building was torn down in 1987. A shopping center now occupies the site. (Then image courtesy of the Humboldt State University Library.)

Harry Kingston's D Street wharf boasted always having Choice Humboldt Potatoes, wheat, hay, grain, flour, feed, gunnysacks, grain bags, and twine on hand, along with fresh-packed butter from the best dairies. Today, nothing remains of the wharf, and the area is now part of the new Eureka Boardwalk, which stretches from the foot of C Street to G Street, where music events and a small carnival take place each year. (Then image courtesy of the Humboldt State University Library.)

The August Palmtag Building at Second and F Streets, also known as the Adorni Building, was constructed in 1893. The Pacific Pharmacy later became Cooper Pharmacies, and over the years, the building has had such tenants as the Levy, Canepa, Danielson & Petersen Men's Store, and Adorni Grocery, along with offices and an upstairs residence. Today, the building is occupied by several unique shops such as the Many Hands Gallery that reflect the art culture of modern Eureka. (Then image courtesy of the Humboldt State University Library.)

The hardware and ship's chandlery store of Capt. H.H. Buhne, constructed in 1858, is Eureka's oldest surviving commercial structure. One of the Timber Heritage Association's wonderfully preserved Speeder Crew Cars, which were used by railroad maintenance workers and track inspectors until the 1990s, passes by the beautifully restored and maintained building. Today, this is one of the only surviving buildings on the north side of First Street. (Then image courtesy of the Humboldt State University Library.)

Fort Humboldt was established by the Army in 1853 as a buffer between Native Americans, gold-seekers, and settlers. It was also a supply depot for other posts around the California and Oregon borders. The fort was abandoned in 1867 and rapidly fell into decay. Today the hospital is the only remaining building of the original construction. The surgeon's quarters were re-created in 1985. The fort is now a state park. (Then image courtesy of the Humboldt State University Library.)

An 1885 view shows Fort Humboldt, established by Capt. Robert C. Buchanan, 4th US Infantry, on a 35-foot-high bluff overlooking Humboldt Bay in Bucksport, which became part of Eureka shortly after. At its height, there were 14 buildings, including officers' quarters, a hospital, a guardhouse, a bakery, a blacksmith's shop, stables, a storehouse/commissary, offices, and barracks, all of very simple plank construction, laid out around a quadrangle in a traditional military design. (Then image courtesy of the Humboldt State University Library.)

A streetcar rumbles down Second Street past the Pacific Dental Company building on the corner of Second and F Streets, which also housed a jewelry company, H. Schulze Cigar Shop, J.S. Seely Men's Furnishings, and several other businesses. Today, the area is the Old Town Square and Gazebo, one of the city's newer landmarks. The brick-lined gazebo and fountains are at the center of the revitalized historic district. (Then image courtesy of the Humboldt State University Library.)

The 498-ton, 165-foot-long, four-masted schooner *Ethel Zane* was launched on May 11, 1891, from the shipyards of master shipbuilder Peter Matthews at the foot of K Street. Not a single crewmember lost his life on the *Ethel Zane*, although in the end, she sacrificed her own and was lost in a typhoon in the South Pacific on July 18, 1918. (Then image courtesy of the Humboldt State University Library.)

Two girls stand on the corner of F and First Streets, which is decorated for a celebration, possibly for the Native Sons of the Golden West. The ferry terminal was located at the foot of F Street, making it the busiest street in town and the center of much activity. Ferry service ceased in 1971, but today, F Street still remains as one of the busiest streets in the city. (Then image courtesy of the Humboldt State University Library.)

The Humboldt Brewery buildings on Broadway opened in 1905. The water supply to the brewery came from a spring across the street. During Prohibition, a staff of two turned on the machinery nightly to keep it in working order. Upon the repeal of Prohibition, the brewery reopened, but its success was short-lived and it closed in 1940. The buildings were demolished in the 1980s, and the site is now a shopping center. (Then image courtesy of the Humboldt State University Library.)

This 1920s view looks north down F Street. The Pacific Telephone Company, which was constructed in 1908, is visible on the left. When completed, it had five toll and eight local operators. The building was demolished in 1961 in favor of a larger location. On the right is the Professional Building, designed by W.H. Crim and completed in 1918. It still stands today as one of the largest buildings in Old Town. (Then image courtesy of the Humboldt State University Library.)

What was then and may still be the largest redwood water tank ever constructed was built alongside the two older redwood tanks on Harris Street between E and F Streets in 1927. It had a capacity of 777,127 gallons and was 30 feet deep, with a diameter of 65 feet. The tanks were demolished in 1953, when the water system was modernized, and a Rite Aid now occupies the site. (Then image courtesy of the Humboldt State University Library.)

This early 1900s view down H Street shows St. Bernard Catholic Church, often referred to as the "Cathedral of the North." The redwood church, which was dedicated in 1886, is one of the tallest structures, if not the tallest, in the Eureka skyline and the oldest building in the city that is still owned and used by its original owner for its original purpose. (Then image courtesy of the Humboldt State University Library.)

A crowd watches from the sidewalk as a band parades down Second Street for Gov. James Gillett's reception. Before becoming California's governor in 1907, Gillett was a private in the Eureka Guard Company and was among those who guarded the city jail at the peak of the Sinophobic tension in Eureka in 1885. In 1890, Gillett became the Eureka city attorney, holding the position until 1895. (Then image courtesy of the Humboldt State University Library.)

The Occidental Pavilion, which stood on the corner of Second and A Streets, was the location of the first Ninth District Agricultural Association Fair in 1899, and along with the South Park Race Track, it continued to be the home for the fair through 1904. It also hosted dancing, roller-skating, boxing matches, the annual Firemen's Ball, and many other events and festivals before it was torn down in 1941. (Then image courtesy of the Humboldt State University Library.)

F Street is well decorated for an unknown festival. Today, nearly every building pictured survives, including the Ricks Building on the right, which had been drastically altered but was restored to its original appearance in 1977. It now houses Bon Boniere, one of the oldest businesses operating in Old Town, and the newer Old Town Coffee and Chocolates, voted one of the best coffee shops in Humboldt County. (Then image courtesy of the Humboldt State University Library.)

A large group of well-dressed men stands out on the corner of F and Second Streets with a streetcar in the distance. In 1888, Eureka City Ordinance No. 111 created the Eureka Street Railway, which started out with six horse-drawn streetcars from San Francisco. The electric cars arrived in 1903. In 1938, due to rising costs, the city started replacing the streetcar lines with bus lines, and in 1940, streetcar service stopped. (Then image courtesy of the Humboldt State University Library.)

Two brothers from County Cork, Ireland, Cornelius and John F. Daly, came to Eureka in 1892 and founded Daly's Department Store, one of the largest stores north of San Francisco. In 1995, when the chain closed, it had five stores and was Northern California's oldest independently owned department store chain. The buildings sat vacant for years, and today, the theater building the store expanded into in 1973 is the only building still standing. (Then image courtesy of the Humboldt State University Library.)

A late-1800s–early-1900s view looks down Second Street, or "the Deuce," as it was once known. By this time, Eureka had earned a well-deserved reputation for being a bit wild—so wild, in fact, that it could give the Barbary Coast in San Francisco a run for its money. Today, very little has changed on the Deuce, and the area of Old Town is listed in the National Register of Historic Places. (Then image courtesy of the Clarke Historical Museum.)

The Ritz Building, on the corner of F and Third Streets, is a combination of at least three old Victorian structures that were remodeled in 1946 into the art moderne style. With its stucco facade, horizontal lines, and distinctive neon, it is an outstanding example of Art Deco design and streamline moderne architecture. Restoration commenced in 1978 and took place over a 14-year period. (Then image courtesy of the Humboldt State University Library.)

Men pose alongside kegs in front of the Revere House and the E. Jannssen Building on First Street in the 1890s. The Jannssen Building was constructed in 1875 as a storehouse and chandlery by H.H. Buhne. It would eventually house the first elevator in Northern California and is possibly the first fireproof building constructed in Eureka. It has been completely restored and is listed in the National Register Of Historic Places. (Then image courtesy of the Humboldt State University Library.)

Possibly on the Fourth of July, this picture was taken looking north down F Street in 1909. The massive Carson Block can be seen down the street, and the building on the right was built in 1903 by a Canadian physician named Rueben Gross, who originally planned his building to be a five-story structure and for it to be the city's most significant building. Today, the Gross Building has undergone a massive restoration and seismic retrofit. (Then image courtesy of the Humboldt State University Library.)

This picture was taken looking west down what was then two-way Fifth Street from around G Street in the 1950s. The Garrison's and Gregori's stores and the Professional Building are along the left side of the street, and on the right side are the Gross Building and the Lloyd Building. The latter was built in 1915 by Lloyd Vernet Bridges Sr., who owned several buildings in Eureka, including the Vance Hotel. He named the Lloyd Building after his son Lloyd Bridges Jr. (Then image courtesy of the Humboldt State University Library.)

This 1950s view shows the dilapidated Weaver Building, built in 1892 on the corner of First and F Streets. It once housed the Wave Saloon along with an upstairs brothel known as the Bluebird Cabaret, where a man could get a dance for a dime. Since then, this building has been extensively restored and remains largely unchanged from its original design. It is now home to the Café Waterfront. (Then image courtesy of the Humboldt State University Library.)

CHAPTER 3

Queen City of the Ultimate West

This photograph was taken looking southwest over Eureka from the tower of the old courthouse sometime in the 1930s, when the town was called "the Queen City of the Ultimate West." The Travelers Hotel, post office building, Eureka Inn, Carnegie Library, and the massive mansion of H.H. Buhne can all be seen. (Courtesy of the Humboldt State University Library.)

"If I build it poorly, they would say that I was a damned miser; if I build it expensively, they will say I'm a show off; guess I'll just build it to suit myself," said William Carson about his mansion. The mansion was owned by the descendants of William Carson until 1950, when it was sold to the Ingomar Club, which has meticulously maintained the building and grounds as evidenced in these images from 1902 and 2012. (Then image courtesy of the Humboldt State University Library.)

"The Pink Lady," designed by the Newsom brothers, was William Carson's wedding present to his son Milton in 1889. After being sold in 1920, it went through several owners before being inherited by sisters in Germany. It operated as a rooming house until it was seized as Nazi property in 1942. After that, it was owned by the late Lloyd Bridges Sr. and in 1964 became the first historic building in Eureka to be restored. (Then image courtesy of the Humboldt State University Library.)

The Sumner and Amelia Carson House, located on J Street between Sixth and Seventh Streets, was built in 1914 ignoring the popular Victorian styles of the time. It was a large two-story mansion with stucco walls and a red tile roof but no stained glass, towers, or turrets. After Amelia's death, the mansion sat empty for 10 years before being demolished in 1967 for the new offices of the *Times-Standard*. (Then image courtesy of the Clarke Historical Museum.)

The Carson Block was constructed in 1892 by William Carson. Architect Samuel Newsom designed the three-story building with large arches, three round turrets, and heavy ornamentation using redwood, brick, and terracotta tiling. A series of modernizations started in the 1940s, when the ornate exterior was stuccoed. In 1958, the corner turret was removed for a neon sign. The Eureka Heritage Society's architectural survey files list the building as "sadly altered." (Then image courtesy of the Humboldt State University Library.)

The lavish Ingomar Theatre was located on the second and third floors of the Carson Block. The new theater was one of the grandest venues of its time on the West Coast. Vaudeville and film brought larger, more modern theaters to Eureka, causing a decline in attendance. The building was sold in 1923, and the theater became a storeroom. In 1958, the theater was gutted and horizontally divided. (Then image courtesy of the Humboldt State University Library.)

William Carson constructed the Carson Block "to create a positive community spirit in the face of a logging and milling recession." The lavish Ingomar Theatre, on the second and third floors, was not originally in the plans. At the time, Eureka had several small theaters but nothing substantial. The plea for a "respectable opera-house" from the local papers was answered when plans were made to include the Ingomar Theater in his new building. (Then image courtesy of the Humboldt State University Library.)

Charles Pyle and F.W. Parker opened the Theatre Margarita, named after Pyle's sister-in-law Margarita Fischer, in June 1906. It was advertised as "one of the most modern and best-equipped little playhouses on the Pacific coast" and boasted a variety of shows including burlesque, vaudeville, and comic opera to appeal to a wide variety of audiences. The theater was renamed the Imperial before closing and becoming the Times in 1917. (Then image courtesy of the Humboldt State University Library.)

The Empire Theatre, located on E Street between Second and Third Streets, opened its doors in 1907 with a seating capacity of over 500. The theater was sold in 1919 and was renamed the Orpheum for a brief time before being renamed the Orpheus and finally the Liberty from some time in the 1930s until it closed in 1958. In 1979, the neighboring Clarke Museum expanded and constructed its Native American Wing on the site of the old theater. (Then image courtesy of the Clarke Historical Museum.)

The Pastime Theater, seen around 1914, was one of the earliest theaters in Eureka to show motion pictures. The owners, Pettengill & Pettengill, brought in the best in featured pictures, vaudeville, and stock company productions to their multiple theaters in Humboldt County. The theater building burned down in 1959, along with the Splendid Café, the Liberty Saloon, and the Grand Hotel. Today, the area is occupied by a parking lot. (Then image courtesy of the Humboldt State University Library.)

The Rialto Theatre, constructed in 1918, was the first theater specifically built for live stage productions and moving pictures and was part of the George Mann Redwood Theatre chain. The theater closed for movies sometime in the early 1960s, after which it briefly was used as a rock-concert venue before closing for good in the 1970s. The building housed a Chinese restaurant until 2010; as of this writing, it is sitting empty. (Then image courtesy of the Clarke Historical Museum.)

A parade passes by the Rialto Theater on F Street in 1941 with the Federal Department Store and the Eureka Inn down the street. The Rialto has been gone for years, occupied by several different businesses since its closure. As of 2012, it is currently sitting empty, and the state of the interiors and what might still remain of the old theater is a mystery. (Then image courtesy of the Humboldt State University Library.)

The Sweasey Fashion Stable on the corner of Fourth and G Streets is seen before the then-mayor and owner Richard Sweasey tore down half of it to build the Hippodrome Theater to offer vaudeville, motion pictures, and musical comedy to Eureka in 1920. The remainder of the stable was taken over by Daly's Department Store in 1937, as was the theater in 1973. The theater has since been restored. (Then image courtesy of the Humboldt State University Library.)

Loew's State Theatre was built by Eureka mayor Richard Sweasey to bring the entertainment and lavish settings found in the theaters of downtown San Francisco to Eureka. The architect was Frank Georgeson, who designed the 70-by-120-foot theater to be so lavish that it would be the "opening act" to any show. In 2003, the theater was completely restored after serving as a department store for over 20 years. (Then image courtesy of the Arkley Center For Performing Arts.)

In 1929, a boiler explosion and fire reduced Loew's State Theatre to a smoldering ruin, but it quickly rebounded. In 1943, another fire left the theater with severe water damage, and once again, it reopened in no time. In 1973, it closed and became part of Daly's Department Store, which closed in 1995. The theater sat abandoned for eight years before being purchased and completely restored. (Then image courtesy of the Arkley Center For Performing Arts.)

This view looking down F Street shows the Eureka Theater, a streamline moderne movie palace built by George Mann in 1939. The original design called for the theater to have been part of a six-story hotel complex that would have included a restaurant, bar, cocktail lounges, shopping, and luxurious penthouses and apartments costing an estimated $500,000. The scaled-down version that stands today was constructed at a cost of $300,000. (Then image courtesy of the Humboldt State University Library.)

Looking north down a bustling F Street, downtown Eureka is seen from around Sixth Street in 1948. The city began as a settlement on the edge of Humboldt Bay, and by 1865, the historic district that is now known as Old Town was already a lively bustling area considering the size of the city. Today, it is a well-preserved district of restored theaters, shops, restaurants, pubs, coffee houses, art galleries, and museums. (Then image courtesy of The Humboldt State University Library.)

This photograph was taken looking west down Fifth Street from L Street toward the Humboldt County Courthouse prior to 1906. In 1926, US Route 101 was established, stretching from Los Angeles to Olympia, Washington, directly through the heart of Eureka down Fourth Street, which originally carried both directions of traffic. Around 1956, US 101 was split into a one-way couplet on Fourth and Fifth Streets. The houses pictured were most likely demolished around that same time. (Then image courtesy of the Humboldt State University Library.)

The second Humboldt County Courthouse was completed in 1889. Minerva, the Roman goddess of wisdom, stood at the top of the central tower surrounded by four statues of Justice and others representing Flora, Ceres, Fortuna, and Juno. The statues were removed after the great earthquake of 1906. The building was badly damaged in the earthquake of 1954 and was demolished two years later to make room for a new modern courthouse. (Then image courtesy of the Humboldt State University Library.)

The second tower of the grand Italianate Humboldt County Courthouse is seen after a fire ignited by a blowtorch in 1924 had left the original badly damaged. The tower had to be completely removed for safety reasons in 1950, and then a large earthquake in 1954 left the remainder of the building severely damaged. The condemned building was demolished in 1956, and a new, modern courthouse was constructed that still stands today. (Then image courtesy of the Humboldt State University Library.)

A pre-1940 view looks down E Street showing the Needs-Williams Building, constructed in 1904. It once housed the Monterey Hotel and an assortment of other businesses. The G.R. Georgeson Building, the first four-story structure in the county, was built one year prior and once housed the Central Hotel. Today, both of these buildings still tower over E Street, looking today as they did when they were constructed. (Then image courtesy of the Clarke Historical Museum.)

Herds of cattle are driven down C Street past the Eagle House and the Grand Hotel, likely either to or from a C Street dock. The three-story, 80-room Grand Hotel opened in 1890 and was the Eureka equivalent of San Francisco's famed Palace Hotel, which had opened 15 years prior. The hotel, which eventually was renamed the Sterling, was condemned in 1947 and demolished two years later. (Then image courtesy of the Humboldt State University Library.)

The Western Hotel is seen with its carriage on the corner of First and D Streets. The hotel opened in 1884. In the 1920s, it was purchased by Giuseppe "Joseph" Perrone, who operated Perrone & Company until "closing" in 1919 due to Prohibition—he continued to bootleg liquor in his warehouse on West Second Street. The hotel was renamed the Monte Carlo, and it had an Italian restaurant and a speakeasy until Prohibition ended. (Then image courtesy of the Humboldt State University Library.)

A postcard view down Second Street shows the Vance Hotel. The hotel opened in 1871 and originally was a two-story building with a mansard third floor and a cupola on top used for sighting incoming steamers. In 1885, it became the first commercial building in Eureka to have electricity, powered by the generator at Vance's sawmill. The building underwent a massive restoration and renovation in the 1990s and now houses businesses, offices, and a café. (Then image courtesy of the Humboldt State University Library.)

The Eureka waterfront was notorious for its rowdy saloons and brothels, but Capt. H.H. Buhne opened the more respectable Revere House in 1878 on First Street between E and F Streets. The small hotel was purchased by Edward George Kramer, who immediately made improvements to the hotel, including building a substantial addition that took over the corner of First and E Streets. The once landmark hotel fell into disrepair and was demolished in 1964. (Then image courtesy of the Humboldt State University Library.)

The Sequoia Hospital was located on the corner of Sixth and H Streets. It was closed and renovated in 1931 into the Travelers Hotel at a reported cost of over $10,000. Because of its location across the street from the post office building, postal employees from out of town were frequent guests of the hotel. The building was demolished in the 1980s and replaced with an office building. (Then image courtesy of the Humboldt State University Library.)

The Eureka Inn, shown under construction, opened to the public in 1922. It was and still is one of the largest redwood structures in the world; in 1982, it was listed in the National Register of Historic Places. The hotel closed its doors in 2004, but it was purchased and reopened in 2010 with an ambitious plan to restore the four-story, 104-room Tudor hotel to its former glory. (Then image courtesy of the Humboldt State University Library.)

The high-ceilinged lobby of the historic Eureka Inn was constructed in a distinctive style blending English Tudor and contemporary design. The hotel's opening and dedication in 1922 coincided with the opening of the Redwood Highway, and while the lobby has changed over the years, the painting *The Discovery of Humboldt Bay*, made especially for the hotel, has proudly remained above the fireplace since the hotel's opening. (Then image courtesy of the Humboldt State University Library.)

In 1894, the City of Eureka purchased 50 acres of forest beyond what was the southeastern edge of town at the time and opened it to the public as Forest Park until 1907, when it was renamed Sequoia Park. Over the years, the buildings and man-made scenery have changed, but the majesty of the towering redwoods remains the same as when the park opened. (Then image courtesy of the Humboldt State University Library.)

A Eureka streetcar passes the Stafford mansion on E Street around 1890. Streetcar service dated back to 1888, and by 1903, there were five main lines that served most of the town: Broadway to Bucksport, which later became part of Eureka; California Street to Harris Street; E Street to Sequoia Park; J Street to Sequoia Park; and Myrtle Avenue to Harrison Avenue. The Eureka streetcars discontinued service on February 21, 1940. (Then image courtesy of the Humboldt State University Library.)

The prodigious mansion of H.H. Buhne, built in the mid-1880s, was demolished in 1955, meeting the same fate as many of the old large Victorian homes that came up for sale in the 1950s and 1960s, such as the homes of Sumner Carson and Stafford Evans. Even the grand Carson Mansion was nearly torn down after the City of Eureka declined to purchase it due to the high cost of maintenance. (Then image courtesy of the Humboldt State University Library.)

A streetcar travels through what was then a very upscale neighborhood along E Street past the palatial mansions belonging to Stafford and Evans. The streetcar lines were all single-tracked, with occasional sections of double tracks that allowed them to pass each other. These two homes were torn down in the late 1930s, and countless others in the vicinity would also eventually fall victim to the rapidly growing commercial district of Eureka. (Then image courtesy of the Humboldt State University Library.)

David Evans arrived in Humboldt County in 1857 and became very successful in the lumber industry. He invented the Evans Third Saw and also served two terms as mayor of Eureka. Evans constructed his large residence on E Street in 1884. After his death in 1901, his widow resided in the home until around 1929. The mansion was demolished in 1939 to make room for Eureka's growing commercial district. (Then image courtesy of the Humboldt State University Library.)

Not all of the larger Victorians in Eureka met the same fate as the homes of Sumner Carson, Buhne, Stafford, Evans, and Randall, as evidenced in these two images showing two early 1900s homes on the corner of E and Trinity Streets. There are over 2,000 historic homes in Eureka, one of the highest concentrations of Victorian-era homes in the country, earning the city the nickname "The Williamsburg of the West Coast." (Then image courtesy of the Clarke Historical Museum.)

This view shows the Hubbard and Adams homes on the corner of Harris and D Streets in the late 1800s or early 1900s. In 2000, Janine Averill purchased the decaying Hubbard house and put an immense amount of time and energy into restoring the old home from the foundation up over a three-year period. Today, it houses the offices of Brighton Mortgage. (Then image courtesy of the author.)